Star Girl

Poems

by

Sophia Michaels

Copyright © 2019 Sophia Michaels

The moral right of the author has been asserted.

All rights reserved. No part of this publication may be reproduced, stored in a retrieval system, or transmitted, in any form or by any means without the prior permission in writing of the publisher.

This book is sold subject to the condition that it shall not, by way of trade or otherwise, be lent, resold, hired out or otherwise circulated without the publisher's prior consent in any form other than that supplied by the publisher.

British Library Cataloguing in Publication Data available.

ISBN: 978-1-9161978-4-8

Printed in England by Gipping Press Ltd. www.gippingpress.co.uk

Star Girl

Poems

by

Sophia Michaels

Grateful thanks
To the fantastic
Elizabeth Tilbrook
and Philippa Stroud
both absolutely fabulous,
beautiful
and
supportive.
Great ladies to work with.
I couldn't have fulfilled
my dreams without
you.

Love

Sophia Michaels

Star Girl, is written for my Mother, always graceful, dignified, and always putting others first, as is her nature. Always supportive, caring, the biggest cheerleader any daughter or son could have. Standing by her offspring with prominence and pride. Having experienced many trials and testing moments during her life, she has stood firm in her belief and convictions toward her exceptionally talented family, quietly wishing all of us success and greatness. Never waiving in her commitment regardless of life's ups and downs.

Family is first and foremost.

Thank you
Mother

Poems

1000
A kiss
All Lifes' Peaks and Troughs
All Things as Before
Style
Back Then
Scatter
Changing all the Time
Cheap Kisses From You
Deep I
Tick Tock
Effectual Change
Worn Out Me
A Star Falls from the Sky
Every Woman Star Girl
Middle Ground
Fabio
Without You
Seven
Finish Me Off
Fit Bit
Here Now
Five Minutes
High Heels
Flower
For the Ladies
High Heels 2
The Housework
I Did Not Believe
If I
Walk By
Kiss Me
Loved to Dance
Magic Lost
A Kiss Proper
Gonna
A New Star
My Seated Space
Old Now
Woman
Weather
Middle Ground Again
My Dearest Darling Linda
The Draw
For My Brother Glenn
Layers
I Thought
Now and Forever
I'll be Back With You
The Beach
All My World
Simultaneous Connection
Weather 2
Layers
I Can Make Something Out of That
Transient Woman
Astronomical You
Moth at the Window
Moths at the Window
Because They Said it on the Telly
Thought, Strength and Courage
Will Always
These Things
We Only
Sometimes on Scraps of Paper
That Picture
Time Bank
Weeping Flowers

Pendulum
Her
When I am Gone From You
Show
The Magic Cat
Our Love
Now This Long Trick's Over

Quiet and good natured, Sophia Michaels' humble upbringing deep in the Suffolk countryside, shaped a steely determination to encourage others to make a difference. Many people are living in their self-made prisons and don't have to. Her goal is to change that, by word, song, and radio. Her poetry being the platform of thought, mind, and human sensitivities. Sensitivities, of which we all mostly dismiss or deny ourselves, preventing us from moving forward in life without the perception of the consequences of what we should have done.

The message.

Prepare yourself as best you can, show up, and do what you can. Plant the seeds and something good will eventually come out of your efforts so Sophia says, even if it's not quite the result you expected. As they say, God laughs at our plans, and usually has an even better one.

Like most of us, Sophia has faced many setbacks, but each time has picked herself up, brushed herself off, and persevered, something that shines through in her many 'gifts,' her singing, her art or radio presence, but most of all, her love of poetry.

Of course, don't take our word for it. Join Sophia at one of her one woman shows of storytelling, anecdotes and poetry coming soon at a venue near to you.

1000

Today
I did 100 good things for you
Went out of my way to make everything perfect and all my efforts worthwhile
So you would appreciate what we have
But instead you picked on the one thing I did wrong.

Today
I made 200 good loving gestures
Threw you kisses and blessed you with hugs and smiles as you walked out the door
But the one that didn't reflect your innate sensibilities you throw a wobbly at then back in my face.

Today
I gave you 400 wonderful reasons to love me proper
But you focused on the floored reason to not love me instead because it was easier than revealing the true you
But you did reveal the true you
Though you can not see it as yet.

Today
I created 600 magical unbelievable moments
But you didn't quite get the magic and the mystery of them
Instead you found a negative to my beautiful positive solution I had worked hard to find for us.

Today
I created for us 800 of the most intimate revelations you would ever be privileged to receive from me Or anyone else in your life
But to you they were just leaves falling from a tree in autumn
Ready to be brushed up then dumped onto the compost heap at the the bottom of the garden.

Today
I did a 1000 good things for you I made sure of it
But you never praised me for one of these.
Not a single one
Instead you bit off my head for the one thing I did wrong.

A Kiss

A lot is said in a kiss
That kiss
It says a lot about the giver
Doesn't it
And it tells you things you don't wanna know
Yet you do know the true nature of the kiss given
It being there just beneath the surface
And no it's meaning is not hidden from view
Though the giver thinks it is
It is right out in front of you
And no you can't miss it
It is not veiled as the giver would have you believe.

A brush on the lips that's not a deep meaningful kiss
It's a cheap reflection of disrespect
To the precious love offered
A kiss not being honoured
A true deception of what lies beneath
The revealing of the inner feelings
Won't be hidden behind a kiss
It reflects what's really going on inside
What's really being said without word
Or speech
And no
It isn't a kiss.

All Life's Peaks and Troughs

All life is a peak one day
Then the next day not
It's a downer
It's a trough
All the way down
Then it's all the way
Back up to the top
Shooting to the stars
The pinnacle
Out there to creation.

One day you'll see the sunshine
Feels its warmth
Admire what it means to you
How this peak of the day affects all of what you do
Every which way
All life is a peak
Ablaze with glory
Adding foundation to your story
The one you want to tell and share.

Then down you'll go again.
To the bottom,
To places you'd rather not
To things you thought best hidden
Out of the way
And view
To thoughts you wish you could stop
Things you thought disappeared long ago
Memories least shared
All life is a peak and trough
So ain't it great that we still live.

All Things as Before

All things as before
No change in that way
Or in any other way
For that matter
Of fact.

All things the same
Way
Your way
With you
As I predicted.

Anyway
And besides
It was all
Foreseen
Before you ever opened your mouth.

Being in your demeanour
Stance
Unbreakable position
Infrangible zone
As I got lost in your face.

But it was what you said to me in other ways
That kept me coming back
Made me stay
Not run away
Scarred and scared
To some far off place.

Now though
I am gone away
Right away
For good
Forever!

Style

I've got one style only
And it belongs only to me
It's the only style I can be
To be true to me
To be true for what I stand for
It's not about you
Your style
And that old hat
Or anything more
I can frankly tell you that
It's about me
And where I am at
I am sure of that.

Back Then

I used to wear the most lovely diamonds upon my elegant fingers
To compliment my beautifully well manicured hands
My pristine nails
Those diamonds shone the sun out of the sky
The brilliance from the moon
The night stars couldn't compete with the expense of it all
Back then
I had this gorgeous plump face.

Smooth
Not a wrinkle on it
Not a line for your finger to trace
I was then in my youthful grace
No crows feet were written in evidence of years passed
Around my sparkling deep dark lotus eyes
When I smiled and laughed
Or twitched my nose.

My lips were full and very kissable
Almost a pout
No wonder you wanted to snog me face off
And my alluring eyes told a different story
They twinkled playfully all the way to the bank and back
And possibly you back to my bed
If I would have ya
That is.

I had this amazing well kept body
As firm and tight as could be
All contoured and well defined with delight
In every place you could think of
And imagine
Back then.
I was all about me
My shoes.

Hair
Fast cars
Big house
And love oh yes
And of course Big love
Big big love indeed
That wonderful thing given to us all
To share and give.

It was a gush all the way to heaven
Every night in the warm dark
I had a statement to make
But that was before
My lovely diamonds were taken from me
The sun got shut out
My life light was turned off
Leaving dullness to fill my space.

My nails
Left unpainted split and scraggy
My care being now at the mercies of someone else
My once plump face having no moisture on it
I am looked upon with absolute disdain
My dignity stolen
I am left unclothed
Often in my own shite.

My once stunning body
Left itself long ago
I am having to deal with this now too
Quite alone
Left with my thoughts
Because these are all I have
And memories
And not a soul to listen to me.

I used to love a glass of whisky
Or two
A Glenmorangie
Or Famous Grouse
On the rocks
My very favourite!
Loved the taste of it on my tongue and pallet
And the hit of it as it slid nicely down the back of my throat
The warmth I felt in my veins as the effects of it took hold.

But now
I am told if I drink that stuff I'll die
Well, whoopee fuckin doooo
Now I am most certainly fucked at 95 years of age
My once gleaming car gone
Now gone to scrap
Sent to the scrap yard
For crushing.

Bank account depleted
My small bed
Stuffed in the corner of an unfamiliar room
Shabby curtains displaying
In the darkness.
No flicker of sunshine coming in
I cry
For the important me that was
The respected me.

The proud one that once was
To return
Instead of being where now I am today
In a home
Belonging to the government
Because all my worldly goods and possessions have been taken from me
By those who thought me too old to handle myself
Thinking that I had not thought or memory
They took these from me too.

In word
Via a form
Completed by some unfeeling git
Recommending
And
Prescribing
That I keep taking the
Pills forced down my throat.

To quiet me
Quell my anger
Until I die
Well
I've got news for you
My friend
You can just go fuck yourself
Say it ladies
Didn't it all feel so good.
Back then!

Scatter

Scatter my ashes out onto a wild sea
Under the wild night sky
For all to see
Scatter my ashes along the wild wind swept shore
To join the swirl of the ocean
In the wilderness of emotion
Scatter my love out into the world
For all to share and hang on to
Scatter my ashes out with the red rose petals for the tears
Searching for a drop in the ocean
But do not weep for me
Instead
Love me to the depth
Beyond the shallowness as you did before
In life
And when you see the sea spray bang onto the shore
With a mixture of sand
And red rose petals
Remember that I am the ghost waiting to hold your hand.

Changing all the Time

How scary is that
Changing all the time
One minute we are youth and beauty
With our nails all polished
Gleaming manicured neat
All sexy and complete
Stunning we were back then
Then we were everything
Had everything
Of ourselves to give
We were good delightful love machines
Popping out the kids
One after the other
One after another
After which
We weren't such good propositions
Our bellies all loose
Rippling
Flabby
Suddenly we are.

Crooked and aged
To nothing we progress
One moment being seen and out there being loved
To the next not being noticed or wanted
We become unseen
To being there
With our wrinkles and maturity
And intellect
That nobody seems to want or has any interest in anymore
Then we become invisible
Once we were someone
And now we are nobody

How scary is that
And it happens as quick as that
As quick as the drop of a hat
The snap of a finger
The years are lost
Gone by
Never again to be seen.

Cheap Kisses from You

I can't spare any more "loving kisses" for you.
Can't give them away as cheaply as Poundland do
anymore as you do.
I don't feel the reciprocation that's why.

I can't kiss you with depth and meaning anyhow
anyway anymore
It's as if you live in another nation
Far out there away from me out there over the sea.

Kisses cost
Good kisses cost
And loving kisses cost even more too.

And deep loving kisses are expensive
But knowing that as you do you kiss as cheaply as you
can
Just one small meaningless kiss after another.

Costs a whole lot more
You see
So I'll not kiss you anymore.

Hard
Soft
Deeply or otherwise.

Because I can't do kisses on the cheap like you
Anymore
Ha ha ha.

Deep I

You know ladies I have decided
It's about time
I did something for incredible me
For myself and nobody else
It's about time
I had my wonderful moment.

I've waited long enough for it to come to me
Worked and toiled
Hard and long
Sometimes blindly
And all too often and many times I have given into doubt
Frequently undervaluing myself.

By those who have no value themselves
So they thought they would drop me into the same slot as them
And all because may hap someone made a negative comment about one small thing I did wrong or incorrectly.
They pushed me by the wayside
Not recognising the thousand good things I did right from the start.

The small good things I did which put smiles on faces
So on I marched
Unperturbed
With no lack of confidence
Not giving into their misinformed views of me
The deep me.

The deep I
They just didn't know where I was coming from
And I certainly didn't wanna be coming from the same direction as they are coming from.
You know ladies
It's about time you did something for fabulous you
And nobody else.

Tick Tock

There is no ring that binds us
Together
No circle of love
No heart shape of emotion
No spill of it out into me from you
No ruby rose of passion
No feel of softness of it from you to me
No key opening the lock
As time passes by tick tock
No sweet scented romance
Of flowers and beautiful things
That I see
But you do not see
The beauty that comes from me
I wrote this in just a minute or two
But the love I've got for you
Lasts beyond the circumference of the very universe we live in
Far out there for time immemorial
There is not one ring that binds us
Tick tock.

Effectual Change

I am going to affect change
Small or large
Whatever the size of it
One or two
Whoever wants it
Will be affected by it
One person or two
A crowd
A country
Or a world
Or two
For that matter
It makes no odds to me
As long as I am doing it
And it may not be you
I give my effectual change to
It could be someone else I give my effectual change to
Because you may not want it
And they need it more than you.

Worn Out Me

My head is worn out
My neck is worn out
My torso
And my shoulders
Both worn out are my thighs.

Worn out from all that womanly swinging
Over the years
And me legs are totally worn out too
From running about and after you
And with you.

My feet are all scraggy
Dry cracked and scratched
As I've not had time to attend to them
Because I am always attending to worn out you
I feel like a worn out old shoe.

And now I am just as worn out as you
I feel used and abused
My good nature trodden upon
My loveliness denied by you
Wanting me to be the same as you.

But who will look after worn out me
If all I ever do is look after worn out you
It won't be worn out you
Looking after worn out you
It will be selfless worn out me.

A Star Falls from The Sky

And now my voice is waking
Right up from deep inside
The words now knocking at your door
A rattle
And a shaking at its very structure
And core
Entreating entrance inside
To your inverted feelings
The brick wall
Ten plus light years away beats an emotional heart
From me
It's gonna take a long time to get there
If ever I do
But what does his heart care about me
Not one iota or jot
Not a spot
Not space
Or air
A star could drop from the night sky
And receive more compassion
Notoriety
Fame
And attention
Than me.
Suddenly, my star falls from the night sky!

Star Girl

Every woman shall eventually come into the light
And every woman on this planet needs to know this
She must come out of the darkness
Into the light
To have her moment
To find her peace.

And she shall know this
Every woman shall shine
In her own light
Bright
As she always intended to
Her time will come.

She'll not hide anymore
Behind the switch
The material things
The swatch
Behind the curtain
The stage.

And the door
Waiting in the wings
Cooking up wishes on the back-burner
For all but herself
Waiting for the applause to ring deservedly in her ears
Which never comes disappointingly.

She'll be the star in the midnight night sky
You'll admire
She'll be the sun you feel on your skin every day
And that won't be denied
She'll be the soaking rain in your face
That won't be ignored.

She'll be the frost in your heart
And you'll feel that stabbing pain sharply and coldly
She'll be the niggling wind
Lazily pushing its presence into your path in ya face
Pissing you off as you proceed along the way.

Wishing you could
Kick it to the side
Like you tried
Kicking her to one side.
Well baby
She won't be denied.

She won't give in
Give up
Drop back
Settle for less
Sit still
Be passive as you expect her to be.

Being quietly reserved
Enigmatic
Now you do not know her as you thought you did
She knows her place
And now herself
But do you know your place?

And who you are to yourself?
She knows who you are to yourself
And she knows you best
So get out of the way
Right out of the away
Her way.

Get as far a way as possible
From her
For she is the beautiful one
The luminous one
She is
The Star Girl.

Yay.

Middle Ground

Here we are back at that place
Again at that familiar space
We have again come around
To that middle ground.

Too many times we have been here
With our thoughts unclear
Our position
In question.

Where are we to go from here you say
Which way
Back to love and hope
From this slippery slope.

To romance and flowers
Where magnificent hours
Are spent in nights of passion
Loves simple compassion.

But no we always seem to end up
Before we can develop
A love supreme
The perfect dream.

Back where all is lost
With traumatic cost
And again the middle ground
Will confound.

Fabio

No flowers
No thank yous
No reaching out
No appreciation.

No kisses given freely
No I can't do that for you
I can do that for my friends though
And you can do that for me.

But sorry I can't do that for you
And I will come all this way for you every day
But you won't for me, it's too far out of the way!!!!
You say
No understanding of my physical weakness.

Of the weaker sex
"Why can't you carry that when it's empty
It's not that heavy?"
"Well it is for me"
As heavy as the things that weigh on my mind and my heart.

No real love shown
Or spoken of
Not now not anymore
Where there used to be.

When there used to be
When you were once full of me
But now you are no more
You can be sure or that!
Fabio.

Without You

Once the sea hits the shore
In its rise and fall
And shifts the sand in constancy
I'll be there
But not to hold your hand
You'll be along the coast on different land somewhere
Far away form me
You'll see the sun set.

Its rise
Feel its warmth on your skin
But I'll not be there to share that given moment with you
Like in that heart of yours you'll not set free
You'll never set that love free to wrap itself around me
But you'll wrap it around someone else
Keeping closed your eyes
All the time wishing it was me
To love the love of me.

Instead you'll love without me being there
And you'll never share it truly with me
I'll see the rain fall
Hear the owl call
While lying in my bed quite alone
I'll hear my heart beat to its voice
Witness the snow fall on the surrounding earth
But you'll not be there to share it with me.

Whilst I in my melancholy will smile enigmatically
Into your eye
Into my minds eye
The trees will shed their leaves
Cast off summer's coat

And again the spring will bud
The stars will illuminate the night.
Unlike you.

How sad of you not to have set free your love
Instead now I'll set myself free
I'll now say "goodbye"
I'll float out on the sea
And still the ocean with rise and fall
And still the sands will shift in their steadfastness
All
Without you being there.

Seven

Seven hills
Seven sisters
Seven wonders
Seven oceans
Seven oaks
Seven brides for
Seven brothers
Seven year itch
Seven decades
Seven daughters of Eve
Seventh heaven
Seventh day
Seven deadly sins
Seven beautiful continents
Seven of nine
Seven days
Seven colours of the rainbow
Seven lotus flower petals
Seven hills of Rome
Seven Sacraments.

Finish Me Off

You don't think you can finish me off
Do ya?
Are you serious
Are ya?
Well you can try
With ya lies and ya deceit
But you have got to be kidding me
In all honesty did you really think ya had the chance
To take it all away from me
My skills.

My beauty
And my dreams
And my super love of the written word
And My Super Love
Kick it all away from under my feet
Sweep it all under the carpet
Your carpet
No less in fact
Leave me without face
With no trace of me ever being in your life.

Only to return to your life all complete
All neat
Loving your arrogance
As you try to hide me
And what I stand for
With your own rotten negative ideas
And words that would often vomit from your mouth
Well baby,
I've got news for you
Which is good news for me.

I can tell ya
You think you can
But you can't
Take anything away from me
You can try
But I don't see the blackness in your soul
Though I know it's there
I hear what you shout in your hypocritical anger of all the world before you
I see pity and purgatory
As you try to push it all on to me.

Well, it ain't gonna work baby
Not with me
It may have done with the others
Who flung themselves about you like comforting scarves
They were your dreams
The ones you tried to control
Because you could not be true to your self in front of others familiar
So you thought you would take it out on me instead
Well I have got news for you baby
I am Super Love.

Because in your life
You couldn't get what you really wanted
From another
From another angle!!
So you thought
You could
Finish me off
But alas you can not
I'd rather walk away
From weakness and shit
As you try to make up your mind.

Finish me off
If you can!
Well baby I have got news for you
Never.

Fit Bit

You fit bit
What a fit bitch
You are
In ya fit outfit
Looking fit to eat
Fit as the fleet
Fit as a peach
With Cream
Fit to teach
Other fit bits on the beach
Exposing fit abs
In ya fitness thong
With ya fit ass hanging out
To all the wish fits
Gloating on
To fit that same song.

Here Now

I am here now
And not anywhere else
And I don't wanna be anywhere else now
For the moment.

I live in this
Chapter
Dream
And universe.

And page
I am here now
With you
Here.

In your dream
And verse
In the here
And in the now.

For the moment
In this space in time
I am here
And here I am.

Five Minutes

Just give me five minutes
Mum said
All I want is just five minutes
To myself
Just five minutes for me
Please
I don't want to escape from anything
Or run away from anyone
Or make a fuss
In any case I can't
I just want five minutes to myself
To breathe and catch my breath
Stand up
Stretch
To dream a bit
Of love and a different place
That's all I want mum said
Then I'll be right back with you
A mother loves being a mother
It's a great privilege and pleasure
To nurture and shape
Those lives dependent
So they'll have quite the mind
And a loving place to be in at that
Because they have a mother like you
But please
Just give me five minutes
Will ya!

High Heels

Flat shoes get you there
Well they got me there
What about you?
Clicking along the pavement in ya high heels
Now I know what that's like
Trying to look elegant and neat
With ya high heels complimenting ya dress
All chic
With sophistication
Outfit complete
Pinching up my toes
Ouch!!!
But still we click along the pavement
Wearing this expression on our faces
Trying to give ourselves graces
All in the name of fashion and the look
I can't wait to get home to take these bloody shoes off
I wish I had worn my flat shoes.

Flower

I sit here now
As many years have gone by now
Day after day now
Thinking of you now
Remembering when you used to hold my hand now
As we strolled through the park now
Laughing
Enjoying each others touch
Hanging on to every word of love
We spoke
Our eyes locked on to each others in conversation
The meaning of it all lost in our fixation
And fascination
Of the world about us
Then suddenly
You would bend down
Pluck up a flower or two
And as you did so telling me
That there was not a single flower on this planet
That held more beauty
Or captivated the on looker more
Than beauteous me
No flower was ever stunning enough
Or ever reached that striking pinnacle
Or stood out in the crowd as much as you.

Flowers
I still like to receive them
Even now.

Out on the Dance Floor

All we do now are old fashioned things
All sedate and quiet
Visiting blinking garden centres
Shuffling along
Passing people with misery behind their faces
Wishing that they were in other places
And not this bloody ritual week after week
How –kin boring is that
I am not remotely interested in a Contorted Willow
Or Princess Elizabeth rose bush
When all I wanna do is shake my tush.

That's all I wanna do ladies
Day after day
After writing a poem or two
I just wanna
Dance my butt off
Swing my hips around
Gyrate them until my presence is noted
Strut me killer heels till I fall off em
Pucker up me lips
And wiggle.

You know how it is ladies
Put on a skinny tight dress
Let me hair get all a mess
Paint me nails
Curve ya brows
And live a bit
I am fed up with the life
All soft and demure
That's too tame for me.

So go on ladies live a bit
Before it's all too late
Before it's your turn in that queue
To stand at that gate
For that won't wait
For sure
Don't leave what you wanna do in your mind
To fester
Where it won't live
Ever
Out on the dance floor.

High Heels 2

I put my high heels on
They remind me of you
Dear friend
The bracelet
The make up
The sexy dresses
All up there together were we
Out there
Dancing away
Our way
To a certain way
Songs pounding in our ears
Beating out the drum
The coco rhythm and song
All night long
Wearing our sparkly faces
Chink clinking our bottles
Wishing time could just stand still
For just one half hour
So we could relive it all again
And again
I put my high heels on
They remind me of you
Dear friend.

The Housework

My life is not just about the housework
It's about me living for me
Being kind to me
I've done all that stuff
Cleaned the f-in floor
Had the wife sex
With consternation and a sigh
When all I really want is to be out the door
Being the woman struggling within me to escape
Off somewhere into a space for me.

To be true to me
My life is not just about the housework
It's about the love I have to give
I can't do that with my head stuck in the oven
scrubbing it clean
I have a dream
And it's my dream
It's the stuff I put on the back burner long ago
Just to keep the peace and every other person happy
But now it's my turn to gleam and sparkle away
My way.

My life is not just about the housework
Making the chuffin beds
One boring day after another boring day
What kind of life is that for any woman
Who set these blinking rules anyway?
Well now I am going to chase them all away today
Because now is that day
It has come at last
It is my day
So no more housework for me any day.

I Did Not Believe Them

Now I look at me
In disbelief
In sadness
My face now reflecting back to me from the mirror before me.

Things I wish that I did not see
How did I get here to this point without really noticing it
That of which was right
In front of me.

Clearly
Until it was upon me staring back at me
Many a year thinking
That I of all people would never be sporting a wrinkle.

(I thought I was too perfectly formed to suffer such imperfections)
A crinkle witnessing age creeping upon me
At an alarming fast pace seemingly
I thought I'd never arrive here.

Reach this pivotal crease
Now I obviously share that space with my ever changing face
Creating unwanted folds I just don't want
I used to look forward to looking at my reflection.

In the mirror
But now not any more
I wanna run away from it
And hide.

Perhaps
I should have used the bloody creams
After all
The potions the frigging experts were always harping on about.

I just did not believe them
For that matter
But hey ho
Neither did anyone else by the looks of them.

If I

If I met him again
How would I react
To his long lost look
I never forgot
The feel of his eyes upon me
The touch of his hand on me
How would I react to his presence in my near space again.

His smell on the air penetrating my nostrils
The scent of which I never will forget
As I stand before him
With that same undiminished love
Not lost.
How would I react to stopping myself from snogging his beautiful lips off
I remember the caress of them well
It was poetry.

As within the moment back then it lived and meant everything
His stubble making an indentation on my face
And I loving the feeling of its sensuality
Its eroticism.
I wish he was here to kiss me like that again
As since those kisses left their mark upon me
I have never been kissed the same since
The incredible same.

So what would I do if by hap I saw him again
Walk by
I would release him of his chain
The one he made for himself
And only this and not one thing more
And he would know then that I still love him
As away I walk into the distance
Again.

Walk By

Don't walk by my house
Without saying hello
Without saying goodbye.

Without blowing me a kiss
Without throwing me a smile
Without chucking me a wave.

Don't walk by my house
Without looking for me
Without wanting to see me.

Don't walk by my house
Without remembering that I was your perfect dream
Without wishing I was by your side right now.

Don't walk by my house
Without remembering the love we shared
Without realising what it all meant back then.

Don't walk by my house
Without remembering that you were the poem to me
Without remembering you were the rhyme and song to me.

Don't walk by my house
Without remembering how together we made each other up
Without remembering that astounding place we reached.

Don't walk by my house
Without remembering that of which we so lovingly shared
Without remembering just how much we cared.

So never walk by my house again
Just come in
Lets start again.

Kiss Me

Kiss me on you way out the door
You know the same way as you did before
Even if you will only be away a moment or two
I just want to remind you what you mean to me
And how much we connect
Attract
And cleave
What we mean to each other
So kiss me on your way out the door
The way you did before
I couldn't ask for any more
And from me you couldn't want for anything more.

Loved to Dance

When you think of me
When I am gone away from you
Will you remember
Just
How I loved to dance
Will you remember the importance of it to me
Or even understand the passion
That lived within me
Will you remember
How I loved to dance.

When at my moving body
You look
Will you appreciate that it's only for me
This dance
I dance
Is not for you
It never was
Or never will be
It is
My solace.

My space
My release from the rat race
My escape
It is not for the want of you
That I dance
It is the want of me
That I dance
So when again you think of me
Remember
Just how I loved to dance.

Magic Lost

No sparkle left in you
Whatever I try to do
Not one iota of interest
However it is dressed up and presented.

No music to dance to
Not for me or you
The rhythm died
That cannot be denied.

The respect disappeared
As I feared
It would do
With you.

Right from the start
On your part
Without good reason
Setting in the poison.

Appreciation faded
As the relationship was downgraded
Just as I had anticipated
This would happen since first we dated.

Drawn to my attention
You did not have to mention
It was noted in your tone
As often I stood there alone.

Taking all the flack
Whilst I listened to the crap
Coming out of your mouth
Words nothing but drouth.

There was no gelling
And no telling
No getting it along together in the mix
Now with nothing left to fix.

No getting it together together
You pushed me to the end of my tether
Pissing me off
And now there is no trade off.

You can be sure of that
I ain't going back to that old hat
To be wiped around like I mean nothing
Standing with my hands wringing.

My eyes wet with tears
As my fears
Materialised
As I realised.

That you never loved me
But at the time I was too blind to see
But now I am not
You have had your lot.

And that will be the end of it
Now I am fit
To move on without you
Magic lost.

A Kiss Proper

I am hurt
By your kisses
They wound me deep down
From the second you give them to me
From your mouth
They stay with you
As you can't give them to me like presents
And gifts
Of flower petals
Share them out.

Their plant is a coldness
I've not known before in my life
No warmth to them
And the restraint on giving them from you to me is difficult
This is clear
I can see
I can feel
The frostiness
And ice
And the distance.

So I'll not accept any more icy kisses
From you
Not know
I now want peace
Calm
Passion
But most of all
I want
A Kiss
Proper.

Gonna

We are all getting older
Getting on a bit
You can be sure of that
However much you think you are not
You gonna get as old as the people you saw and said to yourself
I am never gonna look like that
I am never gonna let myself get like that
I just can't it's just not me
I am gonna stay this way forever
You'll see
I am never gonna change
In anyway or another.

But one day you are gonna look like that
You are gonna change
And you are gonna look different
To what you look like now
And wish that you were never gonna be any different
Wishing you could push back the time clock
Tick tock
But instead you'll wanna look as you did in the years gone by
Way back then when you thought
That you were never gonna look any older
Or were never gonna look like that
It's a frightening thing this getting on a bit
And it ain't gonna change.

A New Star

And now my star
Would you believe
Has shot suddenly back to where it belongs
Up there
And not down here
Where it shouldn't have been in the first place
Being stamped into the concrete
Not being noticed
Its sparkle hidden
From glory.

But you can't keep a great star down
Can you?
You can try
All you like
But it ain't gonna work
Or happen
Cos
This beauty whilst quiet
Is gathering strength
Regenerating her shape.

And style
Recreating a loveliness
Beyond all you have ever seen
From her depths within
Far outside your parameters.
So don't think for one single second
You can ever outshine a star
Cause you can't
And you won't
You never will.

You can try
But it ain't gonna work
Right!!
You get the picture
Don't you
You get the story
Her splendour
Will be great
Her magnificence
Boundless
Her grandeur.

Infinite
Her love
Tender
Her gifts
Generous
And
Her sky
Will
Be
Her
Limit.

My Seated Space

I seat myself by the window now
As it has come to that time in my life now
Where I can watch the masses go by now
In their daily hurry now
To get from one place or another now
Work now
Pick up the kids now
Or meet their lover now.

I can watch all this going on now
From my seated space now
In comfort now
And warmth now
And grace now
Whatever the weather now
I don't have to venture out
Now.

The passers-by won't even know my face now
Won't ever know I sit behind the glass now
And in that place now
As I smile
At all the world before me now
Going on now
And by now
As you do now.

How lucky I am now
To be here now
And not have to go anywhere now
Because I have been everywhere now
Every place and all over the show now
Seen it all now
Laughed now
Sang my soul out now.

Danced my heart out now
I made these choices long ago now
And now I am glad I did now
Now
Satisfied with myself now
That at least I won't leave this perfect life now
Before I move on to the next life now
Without regret haunting me now.

Remorse now
Ruefulness now
Or self reproach now
My seated space
Now
Being the best place now
The best place ever
Now.

Old Now

I am an old man now
Sitting
Staring out of the window now
Watching the world go by now
Walking
Running
Cycling
Laughing
Talking
Walking the dog
Now
Horse clip clopping on by now
Cat basking and stretching out on the wall in the warm sun now
Everyone doing all those things I wish I could do now
All these things I wanna do now
All those things I put off doing until now
And now
I can't do anything about them now
So I'll just sit for now
And think now
About now
And how the now
Came to be the now
As it is now
And I question the now
How did I end up in the here and now
With nothing said for my life now
Here sitting whilst the world whizzes by now
Waiting for my days to end now
I wanna live now.

Woman

Woman be yourself
For you
And
Not for anyone else
Don't be chastened to them who think you inferior
For you can see their own sweet hidden complexities
Right up out front
Though they think that you do not see
But you do.

Go forward to be the equal you were born to be
How strong you are
I know that
You know that
So let that beautiful hidden self be set free
Let it shine
Let it show
For all to know
And all to see.

Don't ever let your dreams go
Not for anyone
Cause they'll not give one hoot about them
And they'll not give the lost ones back either
Or create new ones
For you to live
So
Get it out there
Woman.

For all to see
Be the intensity in the crowd
Show em you have backbone woman
I'll be right beside you
Giving you
Courage
And spurring you on
Don't be still woman
Chase.

Race
To your goal
Triumphing
Viewing the next as you go
Woman
Never accept it any other way
Or anything less
You deserve the best
You are the best.

Weather

I will love you whatever the weather
Whatever storm you throw at me
I won't deviate from my track and path
Our road together
I will stand steadfast
Won't change my mind
In the onslaught
Of the storm
Because we can't always get it together
Together
We do not always gel
Don't always get it together in the mix

I will love you whatever the weather
You can be sure to count on that
I won't throw down my feelings
I won't alter how I feel
About you
Your ebb away from me
And your flow back
I will remain true
Through whatever tempest and disturbance you throw at me
I will love you whatever the weather
I won't change my direction
I won't change like the wind like you.

Nor alter my affection
I won't throw away all we have in our hearts together
The pictures we created
Over time
And I won't be defeated
By the whatever weather
Ever
You think you can capitulate at me
Or create
I am the weather
And you are the whether!
Or not.

Middle Ground Again

Here we go again round
To the middle ground
Back to that same place
That familiar space
I've been here a thousand times before
Now facing these issues once more
Stuff you fling at me
Leaving me here out on the periphery.

In the house of isolation
As you view the position
From your perspective
Your own inner battle introspective
I can't go one way or the other
Because for you it's too much like bother
To listen and coincide
With my questions being too vast and wide.

That you cannot answer with any truth on the matter
So I might as well just scatter
Them on along the seashore
Without giving thought to them any more
So here we are again
To the place we cannot refrain
From to the middle ground
We have come full circle round.

My Dearest Darling Friend Linda

Whilst I remain in reflective mood with you overmuch on my mind
I hope with compassionate heart that you live now in a brighter space than before
Before you left us here in amongst the late spring petals that fell to the ground
With the warmth of the accompanying sunshine.

I knew your appreciation of these things of their beauty and artistry
Of each element and elemental
Often gracing your thoughtfulness and finer thoughts
Caressing your intellectual mind up to the firmaments
Far out there beyond forever.

Shining down from above to those who cared about you as much in life as now in your death
My dearest darling friend live forever in the lightest and brightest reaches of the stars and heaven
Where we all come from and to where by time and living we will return
To accompany you one day.

Where together we shall reunite
My dear friend Linda
Until that moment upon this earth we will dwell in our surrounding space and thoughts of you
I will often think on thee whilst in reflective mood.

I will remember what we did
Those pretty girly nights out
Laughing
Poetry.

Intellectual conversation
Authors concepts axioms and writings
Holidays and sunshine
High heels and perfume.

Vino and olives
Music and dining
And dancing queens as we were back then
Our spirits always laughing.

And here lies one who's name shall never be written in water
But will live in the heavens and amongst the stars above
For all who loved and cherished her to admire and see
Enshrined in a new creation of jewels sparkle and light.

The taking of my best friend by Cancer.

The Draw

I don't know what the draw is towards you
I really don't
And why I am attracted to your inner space
Or for that matter your face
Belying what truly lies beneath.

And behind its expression
I don't wanna be pulled in that direction
To a place I am not happy
Or comfortable to be in
It's as if there's this invisible rope pulling hard.

To bring me back to you
So I can't escape or run away
To hide from you
And I can't get out of a place not holding any dreams for us
Having not a future.

No light
For the latter always being denied by you
And I know you'll never change the shape scene or structure
And one day the cognition will change
And we will fall apart again.

The gritty adhesion won't stick
The thick rope will splay
Becoming warn unraveled
Threadbare and tattered
And unwound.

Being held steadfast by you
Ripping slowly apart
As you try to haul me back in to you
Snap
I'll not be drawn back to you.

For My Brother Glenn

Be the sleep seeing the sun fall
And the wake
Seeing the moon fall
The appreciation of the scent leaving the blooms centers all
And hear the bee whilst it goes about its business
From rose to rose
Dandelion to dandelion
Feel the touch of the wind and the rush of its feeling on your skin
Let the love burst and flow from within
For all the good
For all to know.

Let it show Bruv
Let it go
Let it shine
Let it grow
These stunning gifts come from I know not where
But they are there
For I see them and
I see where they belong
For there's light inside of you Bruv
Wondrous and Strong.

So
Give it out
Pass on what's great and good
What's positive
And magnificent
To make yourself complete
For it will all to come back to you
Released
And
Changed
And
Complete.

Layers

I wasn't told that I had to hide myself
That I was gonna be wrapped up all my life
All the days of my life in fact
All the rest of the days of my life
When I was born to this world
Under layers of your thoughts
And intrusions upon my personality.

My layers were hidden away
But your layers were out there for all to see
Giving no scope to me
While you hid the key
And the truth from you
Deceptively through me
Making you look good.

I Thought

I thought I could polish you up
I did
Make you all pristine
And new
Give to you facets deep
That refract and sparkle in the midday sun day light
Which eventually would shine into my soul
Thought I could gleam you up
I did
Well
That's what I thought.

I thought I could buff up the rough surface
Smooth out the jagged edges
Bring you up to a sheen
Make the imperfections disappear
Revealing reflections of the real you
The true nature of you
Much and too frequently hidden
Obscured
From view
And from me
But then I realised
That you were just being you
No polish there then.

Now and Forever

I sit now
Looking out at the beautiful garden now
Its shrubs pretty flowers
And water fountain
Visited constantly by the many garden birds
I have come to appreciate and enjoy now
The garden in all its glory
Its colours
Its scents
And calm space in the warm warm sun
And magnificence now.

I clasping my old hands together tightly on my lap
Wishing that you were here now
Holding them as tight
As you so used to
I remember the old times now
Wishing they were here now
Wishing you could be here now
Right now
But you are not now.

We would hold one another
Encircling our embrace
In this very place
Looking at each others face
Never leaving each others gaze
Never leaving each others side
We were inseparable back then
We wouldn't spend one moment away from one another
If we could be in each others company.

Away from the world
And from the crowds
But that was back too many years ago to remember now
So now
Sit I
Alone now
With comforting thoughts
Of you now
Knowing that it won't be too long
Before we'll be together
Forever and now
Now and forever.

I'll Be Back With You

I'll be back with you
When the winters done
When the coldness has gone away
When the sun comes back to shine on me and you.

But until that time I'll be a dream away from you
A touch in your imagination
A kiss you cannot have
An embrace waiting in the wings.

I'll be those songs you forgot the words to
Because you couldn't remember them
I'll be the scent you couldn't quite recall
The lost magic in the fall.

I'll be that muddled thing in your mind
All the time
In the shade
Of our making.

Your thoughts always thinking on me
Where I am
What I am doing
The dances we will miss together.

And the beaches
We will never walk along
Hand in hand
Watching a romantic sunset.

With all this in mind
With our beautiful love forever entwined
I'll be back with you
When my winter is done.

The Beach

I walk along the beach
Thinking of you
Knowing that you do the same
I walk along the shore line
Thinking of you
Knowing that you appreciate the same
I walk along the waters edge
Thinking of you feeling the same
As the warm water gently laps across your feet.

I look to the sun
I think of you
As I feel its life giving force on my skin
Healing me from within
Recharging my spirit
My guardian angel looking after both you and me
Even though we are miles apart
You on the other side of the world
Me on the other.

I walk along the beach dear missed sister
Always thinking of you
Whether it is at midnight as the moon throws it shimmering light across the water
Illuminating its surface
Brightly and silvered
Or as the pelting rain runs rivers along the path and flower beds
To make them beautiful again.

I always think of you dear missed sister
All the time
And in every thing I do
I wonder what my sister would think
What would she say
If she were here beside me today
Walking along that warm beach with me
Looking at the sun
Feeling the warm water at her feet
Laughing, chatting and crying.

Be at peace dear sister.

Lots a love.

14th November 2017

All My World

I had it in my heart
To love you
I did
This is true
I wanted us to be an item
To infinity
To show the world
Tout le monde
Amor
Our love
I wanted onlookers to see it in our eyes
To see our incredible love story
Out there
Unfold before them
As we gazed upon one another
Beholding one another intensely
As we did
I wanted each of us to see it
Too
And especially you
Tout le monde
To feel it
In our embrace
To be the envy of all who observed us
Wanting to be just like us
And what you meant to me
And to show them that look on
To me
You were
Tout le monde
All my world.

Simultaneous Connection

Two sisters far away from one another
Walking across the sand in another land
Looking at the sun feeling its astronomical heat
Walking across the sand all neat
Feeling the suns warmth
Relishing in its life giving force
Of nature
My dear sister
Experiencing moments the same
We two being one and the same
Siblings with a strange connection
The phone rings.
"Funny, I was just thinking about you,
How weird is that?"
We both say together through much laughter and a
lump in our throats
A simultaneous connection
Occurs
It's all about the unseen link
An unfathomable tie
An unconscious depth
Curiously binding us together for life
Distance being no obstacle
For
Me and my dear sister
Two sisters far away from one another
Walking across the sand in another land
Looking at the moon feeling its astronomical pull
As we both walk across the sand all neat
Where the connection is now complete
It is now time for me to go to bed sister
And time for you to get up.

Love you lots

Sophia
xxxxxxxx

18th November 2017

Weather 2

I will love you whatever the weather
Whatever storm you throw at me
I won't run away from my track and path
Our road together
I will stand steadfast
Won't change my mind
In the onslaught
Of the storm
Because we can't always get it together
Together
We do not always gel
Don't always get it together in the mix

I will love you whatever the weather
You can be sure to count on that
I won't throw down my feelings
I won't alter how I feel
About you
Your ebb away from me
And your flow back
I will remain true
Through whatever tempest
And disturbance you throw at me
I will love you whatever the weather
I won't change my direction.

I won't change like the wind like you
Nor alter my affection
I won't throw away all we have in our hearts together
The pictures we created over time
And I won't be defeated
By the whatever weather
Ever
You think you can capitulate at me
Or create
I am the weather
And you are the whether!
Or not.

I Can Make Something Out of That

Do you love it
When I can make something out of that
Something out of which
You thought that I could not
You didn't think I would.

Well mate
I've got news for you
I can tell you
I did
Make something out of that
Which you didn't expect.

Because in it all
I saw something you did not
Something you couldn't touch
Something you couldn't feel
Something you denied.

Something you could not hack
Something you couldn't take away
Something that you weren't really bothered about
And in any case
You only ever really thought of your own importance.

And how much you loved yourself
You told me that on more than one occasion
In action
By mouth
But most of all
By your lack of interest in me
Man!!

Transient Woman

Transient woman
Bright and the dark
Sparkling
And realistic
In her diurnal transition
In her determination
Night and day
To pleasure
In and out of love
To give.

And change
During another transient conversation
In the light and shade
Of it all
In another time and space
Ephemeral
Scented
Being a
Transient
Beautiful lady.

Always brief
In her own belief
Of loving colours and
Strong
Short lived beauty
Fading
In a transitory migration
Of love and hope
Beauty and age
Seeing no denial ever
In each and one always opposing.

Graciously
Depicting
Foreverness
And with transient forgiveness absolute
For just then
The transient woman is never satisfied by life
Or complete
Stunning transient woman
Lives in your life
But you don't even know her.

Recognise her
Or give to her thought or space
Your love
Your time
And this is why
She is
Transient woman
Go on
Love her
If you dare.

Astronomical You

I am here to tell you a story
A story that's genuine
And it's
A grand one
An epic
At that
And magnificent
And true
You know why
Because.

I wrote it
And lived it myself
In every which way possible
And my way
I couldn't have imagined the happenings
The chaos
And the goings on
The ups and downs
The doubt that
Ensued.

Feelings I felt
Dealt
It's certainly not just one page or
Chapter
A piece of prose or an essay
And much of it was not so poetic
Nor did it set itself with prettiness on the page
Or book cover to entice the reader to the plain old treasured volume
Of the many books pulled together combined
That wouldn't do this story justice.

This story couldn't be bought in any corner store
I tried that and the corner store had never heard of that particular author or title
or volume.
But it was by me myself, who else of course
You know, every one on the planet has been talking about it
It's a really unique and special book
Surely you will know it when you see it
What was the name of the book again?
Why, it's entitled
Astronomical You.

Moth at the Window

I am a moth at the window
Flipping
And
Flupping.

My wings
Beating fast
As they hit the window pane
Trying to get to you.

I flit from one edge of the window pane to the other
Looking for an opening
That takes me to the light
To you.

But I can't get to you
Because my wings don't beat fast enough
And being so delicate
They can't be touched by you.

So instead
You just flick me away
Turn out the light
And walk into the next room.

Believing that I will die
If you damage my wings
That I won't irritate you anymore
Bother you.

And every time the light flicks off
I'll be gone
Well baby
I've got news for you.

Moths don't die from damaged wings
Instead they flit off to the forest deep
To recuperate in the night bright
Re-charming their space
Before coming back to the light
To you.

Moths at the Window

Most of us are just
Moths at the window
Struggling to get through the glass pane
To the light
Ever enticing us to our fantasy
Of getting there
And to become
More than something we are in the darkness
The place our dreams dictate
Come from
Where we aren't outshone
Or to be
Just flicked away
Without consideration of thought
Suggestion
Empathy
Or consequence
We are just moths at the window.

Because They Said It On The Telly

Anyway
They said it on the telly
So it's gotta be true
Hasn't it
Why shouldn't it be true.

It's what the experts said
So it must be true
They said that I would become
And that I would be the same as them
If I did the same.

To reach this point
And now it's appeared on facebook too
It is a real storm
Now reaching so many more people
This thing that everyone is talking about.

The things that we all want to be
Now feeling compelled to be part of a following
The masses
Not wanting to be left out
Or being seen as the non believer in the group.

And can you believe it
It's been twittered
It's really out there now
Social media hitting the spot
Right where it matters.

Into your cerebral cortex
Your unguarded subconscious.
Suddenly
It has been air dropped into instagram
So it's out there now everywhere you look
You cannot escape the reality of it.

Of what is out in front of you
Displaying objectives
From a small square box
On you lap
In your hand.

Staring out from the corner of the room
Your car
And your work desk
Even in the shops
Snapchat
Backchat

Call it what you like
They said it on the telly in the 1950's
That the square box in the corner of your room
Would control you
Influence your thoughts.

Fiddle with your mind
Determine the lives of an entire nation
Set the patterns in your life
Dictate to your perception
And no one believed them.

Because way back then
They said it was just
Fake news!
And they said it on the telly
So it's gotta be true.

Thought Strength and Courage

This is all I know
Really
How to be a poet
It's intrinsic
There's not a way to escape it
Run away from it
Walk away
Hide from it
Deny it
So I might as well go with it
Get on with it
Get on with the flow of it
Putting pen to paper
Finger to keyboard
Bugger what people think
Not give a shite
For being something different
For this is what I am meant to be
It is a given gift
From where and whom
I know not
But I thank
Thought
Strength
And
Courage
For not letting me give up on myself
For not quitting
For pestering my soul
Into deep unrest
Until the task is done
For seeing life in a different way
Another side
Of me
Bringing on
A different foresight and vision.

Will Always

Some people
Always smile at you
Whatever you say or do
Others will laugh with you
Share that joke or two
And some people
Will always
Look down their noses at you.

And others will look right through you
Some people will always have an opinion of you
Before they have ever spoken to you
And some will praise the pants off you
However small the good deed you did
Before
It is even completed
Some will admire your dress.

Others your smile your lovely features
Your handsomeness
There'll always be something about you that they like
And want to have
They will always want a piece of you
However big or small
Just something to fit into themselves
And some will aspire to be just like you.

These Things

It's just the little touches
And the little things
The minute things
The minuscule things
The nano things
That make the big differences between
The like and the love
The sincerity
And the flippant
The small things
Actions and gestures
Those unexpected pleasure tones in your voice
And the brush of your hand as you walk past throwing me
A sideways glance
A small smile escaping from the corner of your upturned mouth
Revealing the truth in the eyes
It's all about these little things
Bringing on a bigger picture
Of the fine balances
Existing in thought and introspection.

We Only

We only ever look at the bad bits
Don't we ladies,
The wobbly bits
The sticky out bits
The bits that stick out now but didn't before
Our wibbley bellies that stretched beyond the limits
To produce a baby
All the pleasures leave their lasting mark on us
We only ever look at the bad bits
Don't we ladies.

We are criticized for growing a wrinkle or two
So off we all hurry to the aesthetic surgeon for an injection or two
Hoping to regain our youthfulness
For the sake of others
But don't forget ladies
They'll get there too
One day
And they'll all have wobbly wibbley bits
Just like you.

Sometimes on Scraps of Paper

I like to put dates on things and pieces I write
Things important to me
Meaningful
They leave an emotive issue on the page
A tear
A laugh
A joke
And glee
A right gesture
A simple thought
A familiar place
A picture
And a space
A reflection of the light things in a moment
Focusing off to somewhere else
Something I had forgotten about I'd recorded and dated
And I am so glad I did
The memories pop out from the page
Revealing how I felt that day
What I was wearing
The sunshine
And the pain
And me nails all sparkled up
And me diamonds outshining the sun.

That Picture

Every time I see
That picture of me
I know that I can be more than I am
I can be the true me
The one be I want to be
The be I must be
Because inside I am
That true picture
Of me
You don't see that though.

Do you
You see what you think you see
And merely this and nothing more
And only what stares back to you
A smile
A complexion
A refraction
And nothing beneath the face
That picture
Without a voice.

And now as I come to realise this
I'll keep looking at it
At the eyes that stare back at me
Knowing that what they tell me
Is who I need to be
They have been telling me this for ever and ages
But I've chosen not to see it
Or I've flatly denied it
Ignored what
That picture
Has been telling me.

Now though
I look at me in
That picture
Differently
As it
Is about to become me!
Now, look at that picture of yourself
Its expression not leaving you
The one picture that says
It all to you.

Time Bank

The only reason I am here
Stood in this space
On this spot
Presenting myself to you
On this stage
At this moment in time
Is because this is where I want to be
And I have to be
And I need to be
As evening after evening and a hard day's work
Year after year
Missing TV programmes night after night
Girly nights out
Dancing my butt off
And the odd love in
Are the reasons I am here
Dressed up to the nines
Working towards a different future for me. And
Emotively
Hopefully
Inspiring you
For that's what I am here to do.

Day after day
I worked towards a different future for me
It didn't too much bother me
Going without
Losing a bit of sleep
Instead of letting time slip by
Making excuses for not doing something
Letting something, or
Someone steal my time
Pulling me back like crabs in a bucket

Telling me
You don't wanna do that
Well I do wanna do that
And I am gonna do that
So I climbed out
Taking my precious life time with me
As you can't buy it back you know
Once it has passed by
No
Not at any cost
Not a millisecond of it
Ever.

Can you buy time back?
You know
You can't bend it
Manipulate it
Shove it up your ass
Hide it
Pretend it doesn't exist
Configure it however you please
Or stop it
Wind it back
Wear it
Style it into a jewel
Or buy it
Spit it out like a bad taste
You can't get rid of time like that
And you can't buy it back
So however much cash you have got
Stashed in the bank
Remember as you lay on your death bed
You can't buy anything back
Not love
Not money
Not time.

Weeping Flowers

100 Years after The Great War

Flowers all over their graves
Red weeping flowers all over their graves
It's a pity these poor souls could not be saved
These valiant men.

The men out there in the freezing air
They sat out in the cold
They were so bold
They were so young
And on they went.

The Navy
The Air Force
And the Army on its feet
To bloody war
To even the score.

But what for
To be bombarded
Their heads being filled with the noise of the shell
Their nostrils filled with deaths' smell
The swirling smoke did choke.

There were emotions
But not for the politicians notions
But for their wives
These men fought for their lives
To be back home.

Where happiness and bliss is always known
These brave captives in political chains
Were not there for ill gotten gains
But to save a nation from incarceration
Being far from home.

How could their minds roam
To the touch of a silk stockinged leg
When their lives dangled on a precarious ledge
Waiting for the next bullet to f-whiz by
At 100 miles an hour.

In the black stinking decaying man made holes
With freezing feet
Blistered hands
Deafened ears
And no comforts.

God gave more freedom to the burrowing moles
Than to the men who fought side by side
Or in opposition down in these shitty holes
All thought they had the right to rip out each others hearts.

Thus this inspired the arts
Their days were gray tinged with black
But during each night they looked for the gray of the day through the night's darkness
Black souls that visited their dreams.

In these graves stretching mile after mile
In soaking disarray
There was not any freedom to be found
No.

There was no way out
As men had to trudge with heavy boot and heart
Even when there might have been a moment spent in song
As the silence loomed over the doomed.

And still they swore allegiance to their home land
With fists held high in defiance
There was no time to rejoice
Because these courageous men had not the choice

And so the red weeping flowers
Go on like the showers
And the grieving flowing tears
Go on for many many years.

Lest we forget!

Pendulum

Time is moving fast
The pendulum is swinging fast
The time has passed
The hands on the clock go
Tick tock
Tick tock
The time has now passed
The pendulum is slowing
Tick............. tock
Tick...............tock
The hands of the clock
Have stopped
The time has passed
And is going away
Tick tock is no more
The time has gone.
And now time being in the past
Returns
No more.

Her

She left her love on my body
Her necklace hanging from the bedroom lamp
Her shoes on the floor
Her lipstick planted on the bathroom mirror
She kissed as we loved
Her words of advice hung in the air of the
Hallway
As she slammed her way out of the front door
Swearing
She couldn't see me anymore.

She left her scent on my body
Her words in my head
Her beautiful sweat on my sheets
Her smell up my nostrils
And her love in my heart
So lovingly given
But I didn't want to take it
Or keep it
I chose not to see it
I pretended that it wasn't there.

So I closed my eyes to it
I threw it away
I couldn't love her forever
Because the life behind me
Left me afraid
Because all I could see were the things I left behind
And the things behind me
And nothing up ahead or in front
Because I judged her by her past life
I made her suffer.

I thought I knew it all
I wouldn't be swayed however she presented it to me
I didn't trust her
So she suffered in silence
Because I was not prepared to see things her way
My way was the best way
Without shadow of doubt and of course!
And that's where you and I differ
He said
There won't be any commitment from me.

I couldn't commit to anyone
I couldn't love anyone, he said
As I love myself more and too much
There wouldn't be any marriage paper
It's just a piece of paper, anyway
It doesn't mean anything
And I couldn't forgive her for what I believed she had done
Therefore we will never move forward
And we will always be in this place
Stuck stagnant as a still body of mosquito-ed water.

Her necklace hangs from the bedroom lamp, now
Her shoes left on the floor
Her presence in my house is no more
But I know that she was here in my life
Moments before
I couldn't say the words she wanted to hear
I couldn't love her the way she deserved
I couldn't encase her precious passion in gold
Nor give to her the ring of love
Or ever tell her I loved her.

So she said goodbye
And now I live in misery
In a sad place
Within a terrible inescapable loneliness
No one else could ever replace her
Care
Love
Compassion and conviction
Her spirit for life
I tried to steal from her from all of these
Her loveliness has now left my house.

As now I often come to think of her
Her loveliness
Her fresh mouth
I never properly kissed
Speak of her to my friends
I tell them that she is in my life no more
She has gone out of it
She has gone her way without me
Right away
For good
And
She is no more.

When I am Gone from You

When I am gone from you
Disappeared along the road
Out of your sight and view
As quickly as you flick the light-switch off
From its brightness
Leaving you lonely in your night
Where rooted to your immovable spot
You have always been
In as much as I am concerned
Since I have known you.

And when this moment happens
Remember the soft expressions that lived beautifully upon my face
The soft darkness that left my eyes
As you looked at me whilst loving me
The scent of me and the silkiness of my skin
Every touch
Every rise of my breast
Every fall if it
Every intimate word spoken between us
Every caress.

And every sound of the ruffle of the sheets
As you moved about me
Lavishing your promise and passion upon me
Every forceful pump of my lean graceful hips
Every brush of your mouth on mine
Every stolen kiss!
Every time you seek to reflect upon me
You will always want me
When I am gone from you.

Show

Live a life to remember
A life to be spoken about
Make it a memorable one
Make it show.

Make it show upon your face
Make it show in your smile
Make it show in your pace
Make it show in your touch.

Make it show in the things you must give
Make it show in your gifts
Make it show in your thankfulness
Make it show whatever happens.

Make it show nevertheless
Make it show to make the difference
Make it show to make a difference to all
Make it sparkle in your eyes.

Make it show with integrity
Make it show with sincerity
Make it show like you mean it
Make it show its clout.

Make it show with energy
Make it show with strength
Make it show with magnificence
Make it show momentous.

Make it show in all you do
Make it show in every way
Make it show in everything
Make it show in your mark.

Make it show so that no one can take it away
Make it show and you will glow
Make it show and you will shine
Make it show to go beyond.

Make it show to show that you lived out your expectations
Make it show to show that you lived out your ambition
Make it show to prove that you never let go
Make it show that you lived out your dream.

Make it show that when the time is come
Make it show that when your days are almost done
Make it show that you wouldn't leave with the music still playing in you heart
Because this memorable life was given to you to make it
Show.

The Magic Cat

Prowling around
Bush and track
Slinking over rock
Beneath bench
Up tree to the outlook
Onto the world below
No one else seeing you
From your
Vantage point
Your chosen plateau
A place not reached
But only by you.

You are the Magic Cat
You can be sure of that
Disappearing at the drop of a hat
Within the shadows
Without doubt
Or matter of fact
With your mysterious life
Mesmeric charm and
Loud loud purr
But you didn't think ever
Life was gonna be like that
Did you Magic Cat.

And now that the new night has come
For all to see with
All stars and that stuff twinkling from the dark sky
Shooting by
Disappearing in a flash
Less than the blink
As quick as the flick of a finger
So on you'll stroll
Sauntering on by
Regally without fuss
Or commotion
Spreading your charm and delight
As you go from place to place
With purr-fect feline grace
You
The
Magic
Incomprehensible
Cat.

Our Love

On listening to my friends
Deep conversations
About
Our love
As it has so been put to me
Girly stuff
Being put on the back-burner
For years
And
Years
And
Years.

Our love
Given not prominence
Of any sort
Without any recognition
Of our true hopes coming to fruition
Ever being
Respected
Or
Honoured
Given
Credence
Sincere acknowledgment.

I wonder
How many other ladies
Of my world
The one
I live in
The circle
Encompassing
We all thought our love was going to be the ultimate brilliant
Thing
Between two people
Never materialising.

And Now This Long Trick's Over

I have come to my end
To navigate a pathway
For you my friend
To show you the way
My life
Has been;
Triumphs
Of ups and downs.

It's run along the lake edge
A precipice
A ledge
Swam rivers
Rode on waves
Hit rock bottom
Then shot up to the stars
It ain't always been easy
The skies often breezy
Trees bending down to greet me.

Relationships on the rocks
Taking the hard knocks
Unexpected
100 times rejected
Now that trick's over
You'll roll about in the clover
Forgetting the pain
Happiness starts all over again
Laugher smiles take top place
Spreading beautifully across your face.

But I want you to realise

That

I've

Danced on clouds
Sparkled with the stars
Smelt like the perfume counters
Shimmered with the sun
Loved with all my heart out in the broad daylight
Skipped school
Rolled down hillsides
Loved with integrity
With all my soul.

And l want you to now
Look to yourself
The inward hidden self
The frightened person
You have so f--kingly
And stupidly
Kept in the dark
Because
You were shite scared
Of being
Something different
To what you were meant to be;
Others
Made you
Become
And
See
Of
Yourself
As they wanted;
You to see yourself.

My
Friend.
Where
Did
It
All
Go
And
End
It
Is
Too
Late
Now
To
Make
Amends

OMG

It's
Over

And
Gone
Forever.

The end.

Author's Note

My study is the voice of the life the joy and the pain of it, and its rawness. The observation and the questions of it, and that of which made me ask why we are here. To what point is the purpose of our being here in this existence, and frame. What guides us to where we go, and takes us away from what we love and know. What will we seek, and in it what will we find? How shall we deal with it, and the outcomes? Life is too short my beloveds.

This has been conveyed to me on the many occasions I happen to meet with friends for lunch. Where fantastic earthly conversations, in our very small way, took place on the grand scheme of things. To me, we are just bursts of dust on the breeze, streams of light from the sun, romantic ripples on the water, but written in the rain in the end, then blown away with the storm making our mark at land fall.

Life opens us up to the opportunities, possibilities and the fantastic things of yet to come. Yet, in the same breath these doors can slam shut in our faces, barring and locking us out, and from these experiences onward we will forever ask ourselves what happened.

And if I were to place a bet right now, I bet you would say to yourself:

I wanna live, and live I must now, before it's too late, and the gift of dreams are gone.

We are only young, once.

We are only middle aged once.

And only once do we grow old.

A book being written by us all.